Profit 4 Prophet

Nine Keys for Millennials to Gain Success
Through Personal Development

By:
ABDOUL MOHAMMED

Profit 4 Prophet

Published by Abdoul Enterprises

Copyright© 2018 by Abdoul Mohammed

Cataloging-in-Publication Data is on file with the Library of Congress

Library of Congress Control Number:

ISBN: 978-0-692-15846-3

All rights reserved!

This book may not be reproduced in whole or in part, by mimeograph or any other names, without expressed written permission.

Dedication

I dedicate this book to my parents, Fatima and Aremyao Mohammed, and my mentor, Sadiq Ali, for raising me to be a great man of value in society. I appreciate all of your hard work and dedication to raising us. We all appreciate it. I am forever indebted to the support and guidance I have received. I am forever grateful for my mentor, Sadiq Ali. He is a man of justice, service to others, and to youth in the community. He is the author of several books, and I have learned many great qualities of being a man through Sadiq Ali. One Love.

Quotes

"Our deepest fear is not that we are inadequate. Our deepest fear is that we are powerful beyond measure. It is our light, not our darkness that most frightens us. We ask ourselves, who am I to be brilliant, gorgeous, talented, and fabulous? Actually, who are you not to be? You are a child of God. Your playing small does not serve the world. There is nothing enlightened about shrinking so that other people will not feel insecure around you. We are all meant to shine, as children do. We were born to make manifest the glory of God that is within us. It is not just in some of us; it is in everyone and as we let our own light shine, we unconsciously give others permission to do the same. As we are liberated from our own fear, our presence automatically liberates others."

– Marianne Williamson

"Every day in every way gets better and better. First, you learn the lessons, then you receive the blessings."

– Abdoul Mohammed

"When you want something, all the universe conspires in helping you to achieve it."

– Paulo Coelho

"We cannot change the world if we do not change ourselves first.

Take the word CAN'T out of your vocabulary.

Outwork The Work."

– Jay Morrison

"To realize one's destiny is a person's only obligation."

— Paulo Coelho, The Alchemist

Table of Contents

Dedication i

Quotes iii

Chapter 1: LOVE 1

Chapter 2: SELF-BELIEF 9

Chapter 3: CONFIDENCE 15

Chapter 4: L(EARN) 20

Chapter 5: ART OF MANIFESTING 24

Chapter 6: THOUGHTS 31

Chapter 7: LAW OF DISCIPLINE 38

Chapter 8: GRATITUDE & PATIENCE 41
    Patience 43

Chapter 9: FOCUS = FOLLOW ONE COURSE
                    UNTIL SUCCESSFUL 44

Bonus Life Lesson: CONSISTENCY 48

CHAPTER 1

LOVE

Love is the highest vibration and energy of the universe. Love is the reason why we are all here. The love in all our hearts is what makes the world go round. In life, we need to have good intentions in our hearts with every move we make. No matter what you believe in, one thing I know is that The Law of Attraction is real and corresponds to our life. By exuding righteousness and positive energy in your daily endeavors in life, you will be amazed by how many great blessings come your way. Unconditional love is known as affection without any limitations, or love without conditions. This term is sometimes associated *with* other terms such as true altruism or complete love. Sometimes we will be faced with hate from others in our lives while we are on our path to greatness and inspiring the world. We must always remember that what others do to us is not a reflection of us, but a reflection of them. When people are not receptive to our love, we should love them at a distance instead of wasting our energy on someone that is negative towards us. There are different degrees to how love is shown and expressed. Many may show love through a kind act or gestures; however, true love is unconditional. We must always remember that. Our parents love us unconditionally no matter how much we get on their nerves. They still have love for us and care for us. This is how unconditional love is displayed at times. For example, we know we have been upset with our parents at times. However, we get over it and focus on the great times we have with our parents. Love is LAW in the Profit 4 Prophets book. We look at the energy of LOVE as the highest manifestation of creation. When we use the energy of LOVE within us, we can create impact and service on the lives of others. Many times, we hear that if we are not using our gift to help someone's life get better, then we are failing. Always remember to find the LOVE within you first so you can fully experience the energy and express it. The creator has given us a life full of love and we are a manifestation of the creator. Use the gifts and talents you came here with to impact the world and leave your legacy. The power of the mind is inconceivable with what we can create and do as divine beings. Put your mental focus and action into the physical realm and create all that you want. The power of love and focus will allow you to do anything. Walking in the light of love instead of fear will allow you to be open to receive a blessing instead of a punishment. Love allows us to feel a great sense of bliss from the universe. When we are in the present moment, we truly get to live. We do not worry about what has happened or what is going to happen. Fall in love with each second, moment, and minute of your life. Being able to experience anything gives you wisdom, which is the greatest gift we can obtain from life. Giving is the highest form of living. So, share your smile, love, and blessings with others. All goodness will come back to you. Giving is a form of love. When you are a beacon of light in other people's lives, you extend the love within and express it. To succeed as Profit 4 Prophets, we must first obtain total self-love for our self and passions. Love is the key to the entire universe. We must feed our minds with love, positivity, health, and abundance. Since the world tries to limit us, we must have the power within us (which is the ultimate key). The power within you is true love, and this is where the divinity of the universe lies. There is nothing more powerful than you on this planet because you are one of a kind. You must always remember to be gentle with yourself. You are a child of the universe—no less than the trees and the stars in the noisy confusion of life. Keep peace in your soul. LOVE IS THE LAW. ONE LOVE.

The love a mother has for her child is the love the universe has for you. If we are all made up of all material from this planet, it means that we are one with this planet. The oneness and the whole of the world is within you. The love that you are seeking is always within you. The mere fact that there are many different galaxies in the universe shows you a preconceived notion that we are not definite beings. The universe is infinite, filled with love. It takes us as divine beings to tap into the full frequency of LOVE. Love is all around us, however, we must strive to obtain it every day with ourselves.

The primary law is the law of love—all things exist within this law and are created from it. Love is the total and complete acceptance of what love allows. Love is about allowing yourself to be who and what you are and allowing that same right to all others. Without the law of love, free will could not exist because free will is free. It cannot and does not come in portions; you either have it or you don't. Negative energy can deplete us of our true state of being. Our true state of being is love. All things exist within this law and are created from it. The supreme law of the universe is LOVE and the Law of Attraction. Many times, this has been said already. You are all probably tired of hearing about the topic of love. Love is the first rule in starting a business. When we have love in our hearts and toward our business, we will accomplish and exceed heights in every endeavor we want to accomplish. This is because of the frequency of love, which is so high. By being in tune with the universal energy, we allow great things, people, resources, and perspectives to flow to us. Love is truly free will. In business, we must remember to allow others to sincerely be who they want to be. I have noticed in business that when you stand firm on your product or service with utmost love and belief in it, you will attract the energy of people who will resonate with your frequency. You do not need to force anyone or anything to like or buy your product. You present your energy and soul to the universe. And with that, the Law of Attraction will work in your favor. Love is truly not just an action; it is a state of being. For example, let's say you have launched your first product and you receive a bad review, you should not get upset or frustrated. You have the tough love and use that energy as motivation to see how you can improve your product. The love for your future and goals will make you sacrifice sleep, outings, and parties in order to achieve your goals. Your mind is trained to let you stay in your comfort zone because it is not used to the new experience. As Profit 4 Prophets, we need to always challenge ourselves to go above and beyond our comfort zone. Many may wonder why the first chapter of this business and personal development book is LOVE. When leading with love in business, you protect your interests and intentions. Emotions don't belong in business. Actions do! Take action on what you need to do. Lead with the love in your heart to uncover your mission and stay on the course you are supposed to be on. When you are trying to create new resolutions to your business ventures, open your heart up to what you know deep down inside (in terms of what actions need to be taken). Many times, we focus on the frivolous acts in our business. Stop creating problems that do not exist. Don't overanalyze your situation. Just take the action knowing your heart is projecting to you. Open up the vibration to receive what naturally comes from that action of your heart. Leading with love in business and in life is the right decision. When we are in tune with the highest frequency of the universe, we resonate with all the positive outcomes that we can manifest in our own realm. Moving forward with the energy of love will allow us as Profit 4 Prophets to evolve to the greatest version of ourselves. When we tap into the true love of self, we will create a better existence for our lives and for those around us. The universe is our power source. With that being said, why would you vibrate on low frequencies in any of your endeavors? Love is law, and that is why we all exist (whether we know it or not). As Profit 4 Prophets, we must strive to act in accordance with the law of love to uphold the utmost energy, honor, and respect to the creator, our ancestors that came before us, and most importantly, our own divine souls. All is in the state of mind. Our minds are collectively attached to one central source called "ALL". The "ALL" is the universal spirit that is the essence of everything in the universe. You must reprogram your subconscious minds with positive habits that are agreeable to ones that are natural (nature is LOVE). Love is not dictated by how something or someone makes you feel. That type of love is false love. Love is the highest frequency of the universe, which is higher than negative energy. When you tap into the power of love, you will no longer allow lower thoughts in your mind. Also, you will no longer need to love someone based on how they make you feel. Love is the essence that exists all around us and we must tap into it in order to be successful in our physical, emotional, and mental state. One must seek love within, through self-love, and it shall display through actions, virtues, and life experiences. Lastly, there is a great acronym for LOVE: Limitless Omnipotent Vibrations Everywhere.

CHAPTER 2

SELF-BELIEF

Self-belief is having the supreme feeling that anything is possible in your existence. Before we can truly learn to control outer conditions in our lives, we must first learn to have true control over ourselves. The greatest things achieved in the world came from people who had a strong belief in their capacity to accomplish their goals. I believe everyone is born with a strong level of belief in self, however, the world, society, and school systems somehow drain us of the supreme confidence the creator has endowed us. At this time in age, many are understanding the reality of the Law of Attraction, positive thinking, meditation, and visualization. First, one must visualize obtaining whatever is in one's mind. Whatever we put in our minds to achieve is within our own grasp. The only limitations we have are the limits, doubts, and fears we allow to alter our minds.

Know and realize now that within your nature, there are both positive and negative. We must align ourselves with the higher facilities of our minds. You must put a high value on attitude and strive continuously to maintain a healthy, positive, and expansive view of life. It is time to make the journey within to the real you—the divine you. You are merely immortal. You are the universe inside and out. To build self-belief, you must eradicate the disagreeable negative habits that have been programmed in you since childhood. We are all children of nature. We must tap back into the childlike mindset when we all believed we could do practically ANYTHING! You remember that time when you were a kid and told your parents you could fly a plane? Children have the one thing that is important to be considered a genius, which is IMAGINATION!!! When children tap into their imaginations, anything is possible in their minds. They have not been programmed with the self-doubt, false limitations, and ignorance that occur as one gets older. Albert Einstein quotes, "Imagination is more important than knowledge. For knowledge is limited, whereas imagination embraces the entire world, stimulating progress, giving birth to evolution." Self-belief is one key factor in progressing in our lives and creating an impact in all areas. We all came into this world through the wombs of our mothers. Your level of self-belief isn't set in stone—it is not unalterable. We can all be flexible and change, even 'fly'. Remember you were born into this world with no sense of what you could or couldn't do. Then, bit by bit, life started to teach you to limit yourself. A very young child never says, "I'm not the kind of person who could..." They haven't yet learned to limit their own horizons or listened to people who leak pessimism. The strong sense of belief in self is natural for every being on this planet. Here's a story… when Marvin was four years old, he told his friend he wanted to be a rocket scientist. His friend replied, "Hey, man, you are too young." Marvin became discouraged. However, the thing about Marvin that made him different was that instead of giving up, he kept on going further into learning about his field of study, which was science. He started researching and reading books on science, rockets, and technology. He would spend hours every day after school researching his career.

One day, Marvin's father came into the room and his father asked his son what he wanted to be. "A ROCKET SCIENTIST! WOW! You are the ONE. You will do it." said Marvin's father. "Did you know that rocket scientists have been around since the 280s BCE? When ancient Chinese alchemists invented gunpowder?" The story of Marvin shows you that this young man is going to be successful because he is self-determined, curious, and intuitive.

Self-belief is the number one formula to success in your business ventures. The way you talk to yourself is vital in achieving things. Words that rob you of success are, "I can't," "It's hard," and "I don't believe." These words will limit your growth. In order to create self-belief, you need to have a growth mindset. Learn the true meaning of each word (the origin and intention). You should use words that allow you to move forward in your life, such as, "I am," "I can," "I will," and "I can do anything." Remember that thoughts and voices create your reality. Help yourself by being positive and having a great image of yourself. Help yourself by saying, "I walk in the absolute truth in my life." Meditate and pray and keep your thoughts in a positive state. Become self-empowered and get tools in the right way. Remember that self-belief is learnable.

One of the first steps is to re-examine and discard many of the limiting ideas you have about yourself—ideas that you've somehow collected along the way.

We must train our minds to see the good in everything. Take any negative belief you have about yourself and creatively flip it so that it becomes a positive resource. It is a daily task to constantly shape who we are.

Think of typical superpowers or superheroes. Write down the powers you want to have. Self-belief is knowing that no matter what your situation is, with the right attitude and positive outlook, you can turn obstacles into your success. Your power is that no one is created the same as you. One technique used to improve your self-belief is to focus on your strengths instead of your weaknesses. Your strengths are your gifts already inside of you. All you have to do is cultivate them. No one can stop you when you consistently and diligently focus on what you want. Your gifts, strengths, and talents were endowed upon to you by the creator. Become self-aware of what you are naturally good at and go for it (like a hungry lion ready for a meal). We must have great self-awareness in order to believe we can accomplish anything. Taking control of your self-belief will help you in all areas of your life. If you are low in self-belief, it is possible to do things that will change that. You can dress nicely, think positively, kill negative thoughts, get to know yourself, and act positively. A bird sitting on a tree is never afraid of the branch breaking because the bird's trust is not on the branch, but on the bird's own wings. Always believe in yourself. Fear is going to be an illusionary player in your life. Fear is false evidence appearing real. We are either walking with fear in our hearts or walking with the mighty force of love in our lives. Do not let anything stand in the way of the love in your heart and the light that shines through your spirit. We have two choices to make and vibrate on in life: the frequency of love or to live in the law of fear. Love is law.

CHAPTER 3

CONFIDENCE

Confidence is inside each and every one of us. Confidence is truly the way a person carries themselves and how comfortable they feel. One tip for increasing your levels of confidence is to smile and greet new people you meet. This will help you be more open to new things and adventures. For example, try doing something new every single day. When you train your mind to grow through challenges, your confidence will rise.

Confidence is when you are just learning something and keep an enthusiastic mindset while learning. Overall, it's either you win or you learn. We never fail because failure is just lessons learned. Thomas Edison said, "Many of life's failures are people who did not realize how close they were to success when they gave up." "I have not failed. I've just found 10,000 ways that won't work." These statements mean that it does not matter how many times you hit the ground, you must always get back up. There is always a solution when faced with adversity and challenge. When you understand that confidence comes from learning and improving yourself on a daily basis, you will keep on pushing no matter what is in front of you. The mantra to follow to become the greatest version of yourself is—nobody is perfect in this world, however, once you truly fall in love with yourself, you have the ability to do whatever you want. When I was a kid, I lacked confidence in myself because I honestly did not know my worth. The more I started to take uncomfortable actions, the more I started to gain confidence. Whether someone demonstrates self-confidence by being decisive, trying new things, or staying in control when things get difficult, a person with high self-confidence seems to live life with passion and enthusiasm. Other people tend to trust and respect these confident individuals, which helps them build even more self-confidence—and so the cycle continues.

However, it's not always easy to initiate that cycle. So, where do you begin?

A good place to start is to look at how effectively you believe you are handling and performing specific tasks. This is termed 'self-efficacy,' and it plays an important role in determining your general levels of self-confidence.

One time, a young lady by the name of Latifa was always fascinated by dancers on TV. Every day after finishing her homework, she would tune into dance shows, and tutorials on YouTube, and on TV. She was consistent in learning dance skills even though her family didn't have any money to send her to dance classes. This example shows Latifa's self-belief and confidence to learn new dance skills. The diligence of Latifa made a lot of people interested in her. Latifa was shy and very introverted. Dancing allowed her to express her true self. Her brother took into consideration that this could change her life, so he used the money he gained from work and enrolled her in dance classes.

First Day of Dance Class:

Nancy, the dance instructor, said, "Hey, Latifa! Welcome to Hyattsville Hip Hop Dance Class. You will be learning all new styles of urban dance." Latifa was so excited after all those hours of practicing. The first day of class for her was overwhelming because she was getting outside her comfort zone. She was introduced to the dance group and they started class. They started with a Michael

Jackson song called "Beat It." Latifa was shy dancing for the first time around a group of people. She felt she had a lack of confidence; however, it was just her mind playing tricks. The instructor took her to the side. Latifa's shyness came from a lack of self-confidence. Nancy said, "Know that you are powerful way beyond measure and, baby girl, you can dance! So, show us what you are working with, girl." They started laughing.

She gained more confidence and became one with her real purpose and identity. The ability for her to go through the struggles and uprise to success was easy for her because she developed self-confidence within herself. The true essence of confidence is knowing that no matter what you are going through, tell yourself, "It is going to be okay and you can get through it."

Confidence is silent, while cockiness is loud. The reason I say confidence is silent is because when you know something to the core, you do not need to boast and be loud about your skills. Your actions will always speak louder than your words. We gain confidence in our lives by consistently practicing the skill we want to acquire. Students in any subject must all obey this one rule. Everything is learned through practice and patience. Discipline, hard work, and patience is what brings about confidence. One can be confident when going into a job interview, however, if one does not prepare and practice the performance, they will not do well. The more you practice, the more confident you will become in your craft. Modern society allows us to believe that success is instant gratification. The adept student knows that, in order to attain a desired goal or material, they will need to seriously practice patience and persistence.

CHAPTER 4

L(EARN)

The fourth law of Profit 4 Prophets is to LEARN. On a daily basis, we are constantly learning consciously and unconsciously.

Our minds are tapped into an infinite potential realm of possibilities, which I call the subconscious mind. We as people limit our projection by focusing on the lowest spectrum of light. We must understand that our thoughts reflect our reality. Then you see yourself sending signals to the world on how it should treat you. If you examine the word learn, you will see it has 'earn' in it. The more you learn, the more you earn. On average, CEOs read about 56 books a year. This means that they are constantly downloading new information. As a result, CEOs upgrade their intellect. By doing so, one becomes more aware and sharper in one's fields of study. There once was an aspiring actor who was told he should be on TV. He wrote a script called "For the Culture." He asked his friend who works in Paramount Studios about playing in an upcoming role for a new series. The aspiring actor's friend said he will never be on television because he is told that he is not good-looking and gave more excuses on why his idea of being an actor on television would fail. The aspiring actor left with a complete vendetta. Instead of asking for permission to create his idea, he started writing his own script and independently filming it. He reached out to four different production companies about his series idea. Within the time span of five days, this actor, who was once told he would never be on TV, had four different offers. He signed a deal with a major production company to air his series and star as an actor. When someone says NO to your idea, it is just the beginning. Many times, people have small views of our ideas. We should not limit our progression to achieving our goals. The goal is to become a scientist, meaning that we must research topics we are introduced to on our own. Self-research is imperative in order to gain new knowledge and understanding. The motive should be to always want to KNOW. The age of believing is over, we must become KNOWERS. The only way to become knowers is to read topics we want to know about. Not only that, but do not take one book's perspective on the whole subject. One must gather different scholars' work to decipher truth from fiction. Knowledge comes from the source. When you learn, you earn something in return. Readers are leaders! Have you ever wondered why so many successful leaders always encouraged us to read? It is because reading opens up your mind to a new perspective of looking at the world. A person who does not step outside of his/her comfort zone will never know their true power. We are all guilty of looking at the world through rose-tinted glasses, pretending like uncertainty and fear are alien concepts. Stop! While comfort has a familiar flavor, exploring the unknown tastes divine. When we look at things differently, dealing with sudden and unexpected changes becomes easier. People often tend to use being busy as a sham to stay in their comfort zones and avoid new challenges. But comfort thwarts productivity. That little bit of discomfort that arises from having to cope with expectations and deadlines tends to encourage productivity (as people are generally more driven when they're walking a tightrope). Pushing our boundaries helps us to think, work smarter, and hit our stride much sooner. Human nature is to fear failure. Holding back and hesitating to attempt new things are the obvious consequences. However, this prevents us from harnessing our true potential for growth and transformation. This impedes exploring the unknown and, ultimately, narrows down our personality. Taking risks and looking beyond what's easy is bound to involve faltering and facing difficulties. The key is to get beyond that and take risks without letting the fear of failure take over. This is how we keep learning. This is how we grow. We must use the collective consciousness of the world in order to develop ourselves. Meaning, we should not look down upon any religious system, institution, or ancient mythology. All this information is form of knowledge. We must be able to use everything in the world for our greater good and the advancement of our knowledge. We can use everything to our benefit in this world, whether good or bad. In all circumstances in life, try to decode the lessons needed to be learned in the experience. You will never fail if you continue to improve yourself and look for lessons in your training stage. Every bad situation will have something positive to reflect it. Life is a balance. Even a dead clock shows the correct time twice a day. Learn to become an Alchemist. You can transmute a negative situation to a positive one with your mind's power and ways of perceiving. No matter the situation, never let your emotions overpower your intelligence. Train your mind to see the good in everything. Positivity is a choice. The happiness of your life depends on the quality of your thoughts. Your thoughts are prophets to your future. Be mindful of the thoughts you focus on because like attracts like.

CHAPTER 5

ART OF MANIFESTING

Manifesting is the art of going within yourself and using your mind's eye to create things that you want in your life. Everything you need is already inside of yourself. The art of manifesting is the act of using your mind, affirmations, and emotions to create your own reality. If you do not own your reality, you will be in victimhood—always believing that you are a victim of your circumstances. Imagination is the first step in creating your reality at this moment. Start to imagine within your mind what you want to create. Put your energy, spirit, and emotions into your imagination. What you imagine and what you feel becomes your mental reality. This manifests on your mental plane. If you're going to think a particular thought, you must imagine that thought and put the feeling of positive emotions into your imagination. Emotions are literally energy in emotion.

If the picture in your mind is negative, it will affect your emotions. If the emotions are negative, then the emotions you're feeling will affect your mind's imagination, which causes us to create negative circumstances in our life because of the emotion of our state of mind. The Law of Attraction says the thoughts we think the most will be attracted into our lives. We must be mindful of the thoughts we put into our minds. You're not a victim, you're a victorious being! YES, YOU ARE! Watch what you imagine, for you should surely have it. Imagine what is wonderful, good, beautiful, harmonious, loving, and wise. Imagine these things in your life. We already have the power of imagination. Let those negative people or situations go. Being positive requires you to acknowledge what hurts and not let it break you. When you start feeling those negative thoughts or emotions coming into play, remember what makes you happy. It's hard to succeed to accomplish your goals, to make your dreams come true when you allow negativity to enter your mind. "You can't live a positive life with a negative mind." I CONTROL MY THOUGHTS! NEGATIVE THOUGHTS DON'T EXIST HERE! I LIVE A POSITIVE LIFE!

Everything we wish to manifest in our reality lies within us. When we believe ideologies and wants outside of ourselves, we give it more power than realizing they are all a reflection of us. Instead of searching for things and truths outside of yourself, own your soul power within you to create your own reality. The universal law states that whatever you put out, will come back to you in the form of energy. Creation is within us... meaning that we are creators.

Close your eyes, imagine everything you want, and feel it within your heart. Actually, be able to feel yourself having whatever you want in the now and not in the future. You have to be what you desire. Notice how our thoughts are usually in the past tense and the only way to truly manifest is by taking action in the NOW.

The three essential skills in manifesting are imagination, emotion, and feeling. One must have the ability to create a reality or product in their existence to experience. Imagination is a powerful tool because it allows one to come out of apparent reality and create its own world that is not ruled by societal rules, norms, and constraints of this world. They say a true sign of intelligence is not knowledge, but imagination because imagination allows you to embrace the entire world.

Out of all the skills, emotion is the primal substance for manifestation. Emotion is the power that drives the whole world from your gut instinct to following your heart. To dig even deeper, the passion behind your emotion creates an intense desire within you to bring something into reality. For example, if someone is reciting affirmations to you with low emotion and passion, they won't be able to actually internalize and force the energy into their subconscious to make it a reality. Your conscious mind knows the difference between good and bad; however, your subconscious mind does not know the difference. It only programs what it's constantly fed through the conscious.

Your subconscious mind is programmed through repetition, trauma, fear, signs, and symbols. We must be mindful about what we allow in our mental energy. Just like a healthy diet, your mind needs a healthy diet, which comes from the people you surround yourself with and the music you listen to you. Ironically, the food you eat also affects your mental state, and the people you keep in your vicinity who are always negative can affect you. You remember a time you indulged in a big chicken box? Do you remember how you felt after the feast? You most likely felt tired or had the itis.

The intention of what you manifest is very important. One must put focus on desired goals and visions they want to come into reality. Visualization is a key to manifestation. I want you to close your eyes and imagine what you want—without any doubts or barriers to the goal in your mind. We should always be manifesting with the end in mind... meaning that, even though you are not where you want to be, you should imagine where you are going. Be specific about what you want to manifest. In the initial stages of visualization, it's best to identify as many aspects of this manifestation as you can. For example, if you want to attract a BMW car, take the time to figure out the exact model and color you want. Start wearing BMW clothes, going to BMW car shows, visualize yourself in the BMW already. Focus only on what you want. When you are trying to visualize something to manifest (like maybe a new job), stick ONLY to the aspects that you want. Meaning that if you want a flexible job that allows you to travel with the company, only focus on what you want to attract. You can get the things you are thinking about. For example, in this scenario, it would be better to say things like, "I want a lot of time to work independently," or "I want a boss who is flexible and understanding." Then, visualize working independently and having a flexible and understanding boss. Manage your thoughts during your visualization to ensure that they focus only on the wanted. Understand that once you do your part of visualizing, don't use your energy to figure out if it's going to happen, just simply put your intention out there and let the universe decide how it will happen. Immerse yourself in the vision to feel like you have it. Once you have clearly identified exactly what you want, allow yourself to be totally immersed in the vision. If it's a dream house for your mom, look at pictures on the internet of dream house goals. This is so you can feel like you already have what you want. Feeling as if you already have your dream will bring you into the frequency of actually having it.

This is the most vital advice and the one the vast majority stall out on. After you've legitimately characterized what you need and drenched yourself in the vision, you should not ask how the goal is going to happen but have faith through your intention that everything will line up. The most important thing you should start doing is taking action toward your goal, whether it be small or big. Keep taking action. Life rewards people who take action and punishes people who procrastinate!

Try not to fixate on this representation anymore. You have done your activity of imagining precisely what you need. Now you should send the universe a message that you anticipate for it to arrive. Taking a seat for quite a while to envision will communicate something specific that you are centered around not having what you need. Concentrating on not having something makes a circumstance where it will proceed not to come.

You've likely had a few encounters where you needed something for quite a while, and you just couldn't appear to take your psyche off of it. At last, one day, you said, "I abandon this! I'm prepared to proceed onward with my life!" And afterward, WHAM! It showed up very quickly. Help yourself to remember occasions such as these to enable you to not give up when you are working on your new dreams. Incomprehensibly, on the off chance that you can make it alright for your fantasy not to work out, it will materialize. Surrender your vision to the universe and, after that, return to carrying on with your life.

Once more, to show your fantasy utilizing the Law of Attraction, perception is imperative, yet you should take care to envision in a way that moves your fantasy nearer as opposed to pushing it away.

It would be ideal to be particular center around the needed, let the universe choose the "how's," submerge yourself in the sentiment of having, and (above all) let go when you have finished your perception. By doing this, you will have the capacity to achieve your fantasies rapidly and effortlessly!

CHAPTER 6

THOUGHTS

Thoughts are living things. They exist and want to exist. We become what we think about constantly. Your thoughts manifest into life experiences through your thinking, feelings, and actions. What you feel in your heart will manifest in reality. If you wake up today and feel positive and excited about the day ahead, you will attract the energy of positivity around yourself. Your heart is the center of your true feelings. What is important and of value in your life will truly become a reality through your thoughts. We become what our thoughts are dominantly focused on. If you do not feel within you that you are worthy of an idea or goal, you will not manifest it into physical form. In your basic nature of feeling yourself, you should know that the power within you focuses on your self-image of yourself. We need to believe that we deserve the things, conditions, or circumstances we truly desire, and resonate with them on a positive level. There is an old saying, "You get what you give." If you think you can, you will. Judgement Day is when your thoughts, emotions, and actions manifest in your life experience. Everything you're experiencing right now is a result of your thinking, feelings, and actions. Your thoughts become your words. Your words become your actions. Your actions become your habits. Your habits create your character. Watch your character for it becomes your destiny. In all, your thoughts end with you going towards your destiny. Destiny = destination. We all have different destinations.

Your thoughts are a magnet that will provide focus and growth. Be conscious about your thinking because the law of the universe are mental thoughts that we dominantly focus on.

Thoughts are the gift of the divine power within us. Look around you. All the great things and ideas that come from our very own eyes have all come through thoughts. From now on, you should know that thoughts are powerful, and creation resides within thoughts, ideas, and actions. We live in a created universe, so our thoughts are fragments of us. What we think, so shall we reap.

Get rid of doubt and fear of things going wrong. The intention behind your thoughts is what is creating your life experiences. The truth is… we must act as if what we intend to manifest is already in our reality. Cancel out your negative thoughts and completely eliminate thoughts of limitations, doubts, and fears of yourself achieving that reality. Remember you are a MASTERPIECE OF THE MOST HIGH. The temple of the Most High lies within all of us. It is time for us to take our power back into our hands and believe in the greatness of our existence.

Thoughts are why everything is in existence. Before you were even born, you were in the thoughts of your parents. The first principle of Mentalism is All is in the Mind; The Universe is Mental. With that being said, we can see if all our perceptions, thinking, and emotions start and end in our minds. In order to ascend through the limitations, we place in our minds, we should imagine the possibilities of our great thoughts manifesting. Why focus on a thought that does not cater to improving your well-being?

Our minds may be linked to a garden, which will be cultivated or allowed to roam freely. We do not attract that which we want, but that of what we are. Good thoughts and actions can never produce bad results—bad thoughts and actions can never produce good results. This is a Law of Cause and Effect. You will always get what you give.

Your body is a servant to your mind. Your thoughts will affect your health and body. Disease and health are like life circumstances—they are based on thoughts. Low vibrations and sickly thoughts will express themselves throughout the body.

Know that and realize now, within nature, there is positive and negative. You must—and we stress must—use only the positive thoughts to realign with our God Self or High Self. We should place a high value on the attitude of our thoughts and strive continuously to maintain a healthy, positive, enhanced attitude toward life.

We must break free of disagreeable negative habits that have been acquired throughout one's lifetime. You must reprogram your subconscious mind to positive habits and thoughts in order to manifest a positive life of abundance, success, and achievement that is within all of us. You are divinity, you are Gods and Goddesses. The temple of the Most High lies within. You are divine beings of the universe made by stardust. Meaning you have a right to shine bright. The stars in the sky—you are a reflection of that which you see outside of this world. The same theory goes for your thoughts. The thoughts that your mind dominantly focuses on will create your own reality. All that we are arises from our thoughts. With our thoughts, we create the world around us. Speak and act with an impure mind and trouble will follow. The same goes for shifting your thoughts to positivity. The greatest way to shift your energy from negative to positive is to first be GRATEFUL for what you already have. This will bring a tremendous shift to your energy and change your mindset.

Playing small and thinking negatively will lead you to live an unfulfilled life because of the weeds you have sowed in your mind. Affirmations help many leaders to program their subconscious minds through repetition to affirm all the great things one can be. You are truly the master of your own thoughts, and no one can control what you think and how you think. Become the master of your destiny by aligning with thoughts that are agreeable to the greater good and abundance of your life.

Mind Excise 1: Monitor your thoughts. Do not attach yourself to them. Your thoughts always create your reality, so consciously monitor your thought patterns. If they are on a negative or low energy thought pattern like worrying, complaining, and blaming others, you will block yourself from being the greatest version of yourself.

Your intuitive nature is very powerful. Whatever you hear and truly desire, you will feel those thoughts manifest in your life. For

For example, if you truly desire to get healthy and be in shape, you will focus on thoughts based on fitness, exercising, health, and things related to being healthy and getting in shape. Everything we want all starts with a mindset, which thought stems from. Health is a result of positive and correct thinking.

Let go of all limitations of doubt, worry, fear, anxiety, and negative thoughts that will hold you back from becoming great and manifesting greatness! The ability to dictate our circumstances due to thought precedes action. Our thoughts must encompass our purpose. Knowing that our thoughts are things, we can manifest our fantasies into reality through our actions. We must focus on the object of our desire, act accordingly, and we will receive what we've toiled for understanding. Also, we can achieve a frequency that we will transmute energy into matter.

The workshop of the MIND is a place where things are of THOUGHT. As we wish to become, we must act that way now. You can polarize, meaning fix your mind on certain thoughts, and you will only attract those types of people into your life who think the same way because you are giving off the same vibrations of thought. When we live in the Nature of Divinity, we produce more prosperity, wealth, health and an infinite abundance of ideas, love, and well-being for ourselves and those amongst us. Your mind is a magnet that draws to it thoughts that keep up with your conscious and subconscious mind. Thought comes first in the find, then feeling, and then desire to execute the thought. Then your formula will be will power in order to manifest your thoughts into physical reality. Thoughts become things. You create magic any time you create a thought, however, the goal is to create a thought and make it work in your best interest, and that is your true master. We must have self-control over our thoughts. You are your thoughts. If we cannot control our thoughts, we cannot control ourselves.

CHAPTER 7

LAW OF DISCIPLINE

Law of discipline. The reason why we call it law is because, in order for one to achieve any amount of success in life, one must have self-discipline. Without self-discipline, great tasks cannot be accomplished. Discipline makes your life easier, helps organize your life, and encourages you to stay committed after you already have something that you are going to do. Focus on your path with diligence and discipline.

Discipline makes a craft perfect. Discipline helps us make better health options when it comes to what we put into our bodies. What we plant in our minds must return to us. We must be mindful of what we plant into our minds because we can alter our reality from our thoughts.

Step one, figure out your strengths and weaknesses in order to improve your life. Own up to your flaws because you cannot overcome

Unless you can measure where you are. Discipline is vital to becoming the best version of yourself. Discipline is not a natural behavior; it is a learned behavior just like goals and accomplishments. It requires practice, repetition, and hard work.

Stay committed to your goals by always taking the first step. Persistence is the key that will create a sense of knowing or what some call "faith".

Procrastination is a deadly disease. Whenever you keep putting things off that are vital to your purpose and DESTINY, you are fooling yourself because time only exists in the NOW. The biggest enemy you must deal with is yourself. When you know you need to get things done promptly, act with a sense of urgency because the only time that exists is NOW. If we constantly think we can wait forever to get things done, nothing will get done in the world. Men and women need to act with a sense of urgency with their destiny. Many of us start things and do not finish them.

Cancel out all the programs of undisciplined actions. Focus on the energy of discipline, courage, and actions. Actions should be taken daily in order to achieve our dreams. Dreams without goals are dead. You must have big goals with the proper intention of achieving them. This is where goals come into place. At the heart of any

A successful person is self-discipline. Whether it's success in their personal lives or their professional lives, it all starts with an inherent ability for self-control through discipline. Your thoughts. Your emotions. Your behaviors. And your habits. All of them must be kept in check. If you want to achieve those lofty goals you set, understanding how to discipline yourself is a key ingredient. It is the recipe for success. But self-discipline isn't something new. Do not get it wrong. It is not about being perfect. It is about the effort. And when you bring that consistent effort every single day, that is where transformation happens, and change occurs. Consistent action creates consistent results. Remember, consistency gains respect. Jim Rohn claimed, "Discipline is the bridge between goals and accomplishment." We must train our minds to put our priorities first before our desires.

CHAPTER 8

GRATITUDE & PATIENCE

Gratitude is the key to happiness. One must be grateful for what they have. People will be put in a position to receive more than what they have when they are grateful. Zig Ziglar states, "Gratitude is the healthiest of all human emotions. The more you express gratitude for what you have, the more likely you will have even more to express gratitude for."

Learn to be thankful for what you already have while you pursue your goals and dreams. If you cannot be thankful and have gratitude for where you are in this exact moment, why should you be able to receive more in life if you do not appreciate what you have already?

Gratitude is essential to creating more success and opportunities in your life. The energy of gratitude will shift your life tremendously. The more gratitude you feel and express, the more likely you are to attract the things you desire into your life. "Be thankful for what you have; you'll end up having more. If you concentrate on what you don't have, you will never, ever have enough." — Oprah Winfrey

Feeling thankful is a positive feeling and your heart should be open to it. When you are grateful for something, you have acknowledged its reality. You can create a gratitude state by basically saying, "Thank you." Say it so anyone can hear. Also, say it to other individuals and to yourself. You can even take some time without anyone else to rehash, "Thank you," particularly out loud. Saying it again and again as a mantra will inevitably encourage you to feel thankful for everything. Gratitude blesses you. It opens you up so that more can come in. It literally expands the vibrational space around you. When you're living in that expansive space, more of everything will flow into your life.

You can create a gratitude journal. Write thank-you letters to five people who made a profound impact in your life and take a gratitude walk with your loved ones or by yourself. Focus on all that you are truly thankful for; such as your health, family, friends, home, food, and all that is essential to living a great life. Be thankful!

Gratitude for the absence of things is just as important as feeling grateful for the presence of things. We tend to look for situations, people, or possessions we can be grateful for. However, you can also practice having a consciousness of gratitude for things that no longer exist—for instance, circumstances or individuals that have been removed from our lives by our own will, or by fate, or by divine intervention.

Patience

There is an African proverb that goes something like this, "Anything great done in the world took a discipline of patience. Patience is truly a virtue of life. The greatest thing done in this world took a level of patience." Look around. Everything great in the world took a level of patience, dedication, and persistence to create it. For example, for your iPhone. To be made, all the technological parts must be manufactured and then put into the right part of the phone in order for it to work. All of these steps take patience. It takes six months to build a Rolls Royce and 13 hours to build a Toyota. In order to achieve greatness in life, one will need a level of patience to outlast the journey. The journey never stops. It is always a marathon. It is just the beginning of your life works, so let patience be the virtue while you take action to get where you want to be.

CHAPTER 9

FOCUS = FOLLOW ONE COURSE UNTIL SUCCESSFUL

FOCUS, FOCUS, FOCUS! Follow one course until successful. In order to achieve great works, one must focus on one goal at a time. Desiderius Erasmus Quotes, "In the land of the blind, the one-eyed man is king." When you have many tabs open on the browser, you still have to focus on one webpage at a time. Our minds can sometimes be cluttered with many different projects, and we want to complete all of them at once. However, in order to succeed, we must master one field at a time. This requires attention and focus to grasp the material of the field. Then the information must be applied/implemented in order to receive results. I know we have been taught to multi-task because it helps us to save time to get more things done. However, this is not 100% true. When you are multitasking, you are doing two or more things at one time. This is not allowing you to effectively focus on one task at a time. FOLLOW ONE COURSE UNTIL SUCCESSFUL! YOU ARE IN CONTROL OF YOUR TIME! TIME IS THE MOST VALUABLE ASSET WE HAVE ON EARTH.

Focus means being able to pay attention to your plan and control the everyday distractions that life puts in your path. Of course, there will be times when unforeseen things happen, but you will be more prepared and confident to deal with them. It would be foolish to suggest that no one experiences insecurities and doubts. Feel them and learn from them. Always be mindful of your plan and follow it. But be mindful that it might not go according to your initial plan. That doesn't mean that you won't find a way to resolve it. It's for you to have a contingency in place.

Being more focused on one thing at a time will allow you to be more positive. It allows you to be sure about what you know and what you trust you can accomplish. Energy and being more idealistic will support your objectives. Your mental state will drive your assurance, which will empower you to accomplish your aspirations. Believe in yourself and reveal to yourself that you can do it. The little victories will drive the challenges that will empower you to manage the greater undertakings. Recognize your diligent work by having an arrangement and coordinated concentration to accomplish your objectives. This will provide you with an establishment for your future successes.

Accomplishing many things at one time at any given moment is an awesome method to end up busier and it's typically an additionally captivating method for working. When we do portion out doing numerous things in the meantime, the mind is more empowered, and it discharges more dopamine (a chemical compound within the brain that produces joy). In any case, many studies have demonstrated that while multitasking can be animating, and may even influence us to feel more profitable, it perpetually makes us less productive.

Focus is the opposite of multitasking and it's better in virtually every way. Our brains may initially resist single tasking because it's less stimulating. But working on one thing at a time lets us dive deeper and do a better job at each task. This way, we don't have to spread our time, attention, and energy—the three ingredients of productivity—across many things at once. Single tasking lets us create more attentional space around our work at the moment. This lets us think deeper, make more connections, work more creatively, and find more meaning in the work. If you think back to a great productive day, you likely weren't doing a thousand things at once. Chances are, you were working on just one task and spending an inordinate amount of time, attention, and energy on it. While it takes time and energy to adapt to being less stimulated throughout the day, it's easily worth it. Single-tasking will even let us build up our attention muscle, which helps how much control we have over where we direct our attention.

You create your reality. Abundance is our birthright. Be open and receptive to the abundance and wealth in the universe. If you think from a place of wealth and riches, you will surely create that. Your ideas are your greatest assets. Take action because your assets will always pay off. If your mind can conceive it, you can achieve it. You have the power to do the most incredible things with your mind because your mind has unlimited power. Focus on your strengths and not your weakness. Create solutions and not problems. Train your mind to already achieve goals through visualization and imagining yourself in the position you want. Use affirmations to reprogram your subconscious into believing whatever you want to create.

BONUS LIFE LESSON

e

CONSISTENCY

Consistency is a virtue in life in order to achieve greatness. Consistent action creates consistent results. In order to keep progressive realization of our goals and dreams, we need to be consistent in our actions toward our task. In order to keep focused and keep moving, you first need a goal. Once you have a goal, you must be committed to your destination. Consistency is the master key to success. The ability to make yourself do what you should do whether you feel like it or not. Do something every day related to your goal in order to increase the skill level of your craft. Once you believe in what you are doing, you will be consistent in doing your work. If you want to achieve anything of value and meaning in your life, then you need to be consistent. This holds true in business and in relationships. If something isn't working in your life, ask yourself, "Have I been giving it consistent attention, energy, and time?"

Consistency is about building small, empowering habits and rituals that you partake in every single day that keep you focused on your highest priorities and goals. It, therefore, essentially comes down to your ability to hold yourself accountable for the daily choices you make with no excuses or complaints. You and you alone are accountable for what you do and what you fail to do. All responsibility lies solely in your hands.

To be consistent means to focus on the present moment while maintaining a long-term view that helps you measure your results and the impact of your daily actions. With this regular feedback in your hands, you are better able to learn from your failures and mistakes. This will help you effectively alter your course of action where required. Consistency is, therefore, all about repetition. It's about repeating the same actions, habits, and rituals over and over again, gaining feedback from these actions, and adjusting them accordingly to help you stay on track as you work towards your goal. And that, in essence, is the difference between success and failure in any field of endeavor and the key to high levels of achievement.

www.ingramcontent.com/pod-product-compliance
Lightning Source LLC
Chambersburg PA
CBHW070950180426
43194CB00041B/2032